G000141247

THE LITTLE MEDITERRANEAN FOOD BOOK

Rena Salaman

PIATKUS

Other titles in this series include

The Little Green Avocado Book
The Little Garlic Book
The Little Pepper Book
The Little Lemon Book
The Little Strawberry Book
The Little Mushroom Book
The Little Bean Book
The Little Rice Book
The Little Tea Book
The Little Coffee Book
The Little Curry Book
The Little Chocolate Book

© 1986 Judy Piatkus (Publishers) Limited

British Library Cataloguing in Publication Data
Salaman, Rena
The little Mediterranean food book.
1. Cookery, Mediterranean
I. Title
641.3′009182′2   TX725.M35
ISBN 0-86188-548-1

Drawings by Linda Broad
Designed by Ken Leeder
Cover illustrated by Lynne Robinson

Phototypeset in 10/11pt Linotron Plantin by
Phoenix Photosetting, Chatham
Printed and bound in Great Britain by
The Bath Press, Avon

CONTENTS

MEDITERRANEAN — THE ADJECTIVE

The term 'Mediterranean' has various connotations, but these always produce the same images.

– When applied to the weather, brilliant sunshine floods our eyes, unnaturally shadowless and unique in its luminosity.

– Applied to colour, it describes primarily the intense electrifying blue of the Mediterranean sky with the dark green of slender cypress tops swaying against it.

– Applied to people, the connotations are of exuberance, warmth, vibrant emotions (perhaps a trifle exaggerated at times), hospitality and immediacy. If applied to the male of the species in particular, I am afraid the connotations are twofold: chauvinistic and alas . . . oversexed. (Try sitting alone on the steps at the Piazza d'Espagna in Rome or at a seafront Kafenion on an Aegean island.)

– Applied to markets, it brings images of clustered stalls with vibrant produce spilling everywhere: the cries, the noises, the bargaining, the disputing, the gesticulating. It is a magnificent set for a magnificent performance!

– Applied to families, it has even acquired sociological notions; the extended but the tightly-knit family, the self-contained nucleus which is often self-supportive, both physically and emotionally.

– Applied to food, it brings to mind colourful combinations of vegetables adorned with scarlet tomatoes and the *bête noir* of Tobias Smollett's Mediterranean experiences, garlic. Parading in an extravagant sequence are fiercely purple aubergines, youthful, green, rose-petal-shaped artichokes, pale, bashful courgettes and many more, all permeated with the aromas of the hills.

But how can one adjective be applied unilaterally to a handful of different countries, each with its distinct language and traditions, and with rich, diverse cultures and religions? Arabs, Turks, Greeks and Latins! What is the unifying factor over this heterogeneous gathering?

Primarily, it is the sea, the Mediterranean, which is not strictly one sea but made up of the Aegean, the Adriatic, the Ionian, the Ligurian and the Tyrrhenian (Corsica and Sardinia) Seas. Over this sea voyagers sailed, conquerors conquered, preachers preached, merchants bartered and crusaders preached and conquered at the same time. The sea inspired and supported the constant exchanges within this geographical extravagance, bordered by the olive tree in the north and the palm in the south.

The second unifying factor (but not second in importance) is the climate that dictates the rhythm and quality of life. Nowhere else in the world are seasons so distinct: two mellow and two full-hearted ones, in the winter mild and wet, in summer generous in warmth and sunshine.

MEDITERRANEAN FOOD
THROUGH HISTORY

C an one speak of Mediterranean food? Is there a homogeneous culinary culture that one expects to find at a Mediterranean table?

The culturally rich communities around the Mediterranean have been in contact for six or seven thousand years. The Greeks marched to the East as far as India, where they must have been surprised at least by the exotic produce: rice, aubergines, spinach and a golden array of fruit, never encountered before!

They sailed to the West and colonised both the north and south coasts, Sicily, Carthage and Marseilles. Even nowadays there is an autonomous Greek church at Palermo, with a Greek speaking (archaic maybe) congregation, peasant songs and the full array of Greek customs and superstitions.

As Greek power declined, the Roman empire rose and in their turn the Romans took over almost the entire Mediterranean, until in AD 476 the last Roman emperor, Romulus Augustulus, was overthrown by the Barbarians.

By this time, Byzantine power had acquired impetus and, sailing from their splendid palaces and churches in Constantinople, the Byzantines, in their turn, colonised Sicily, Italy and North Africa.

The Arab invasions started along the southern Mediterranean coast during the 7th century. Though unsuccessful at first, Alexandria, Cyprus, Rhodes, Crete, Carthage fell one after the other. The incursions continued in waves through the 8th and 9th centuries and the Arabs eventually controlled part of the Iberian peninsula and Sicily for 800 years. By about 843, Arab piracy was a constant menace. All the big islands experienced the Saracen touch and modern songs still recall and lament.

In 1096, the first Crusade began, with the purpose of bringing the Gospel to the East, where, ironically, it had originated. And from the 11th to the 14th century, when the movement declined, the Crusaders must have been astounded by the produce and foods they found in their travels, which they brought back to Western Europe in their saddlepacks.

In May 1453, Constantinople, the glittering city, fell to the armies of Mohammed II; Ottoman power rose, and with all its splendour Ottoman culture spread from East to West, conquering and colonising as far as Sicily. The Ottomans were held at bay by one significant blow only, the battle of Lepanto. Christian alliances were formed by the Spaniards, the Venetians and Romans and on 7 October 1571 their fleets met the Ottoman and Egyptian fleets outside Lepanto, the modern city of Nafpactos on the western coast of Greece, where the Christian victory was overwhelming.

Despite the journeys of colonising Greeks and Romans, Levantine merchants, Byzantine silk traders, invading Arabs, Saracen pirates and marching crusaders, Mediterranean cooking was not to take its familiarly recognisable shape until later, from the 16th century onwards. Many of its ingredients were already present and flourishing; others were yet to be introduced.

Some of the great favourites which are automatically associated with the Mediterranean cuisine, such as aubergines, spinach, rice, colocasia, lemons, tangerines, bergamots and water-melons, were brought from Indochina by the Arabs and spread westwards through the Islamic conquests.

Along with the vegetables, the Arabs brought new spices to go with them, such as cinnamon, allspice and ginger. These, together with cummin and black pepper, already popular in the ancient world, are to be found in varying degrees in Mediterranean cooking.

In the 15th century, the discovery of the New World by the Spaniards and the Portuguese introduced Mediterranean cuisine to some of its other indispensable participants: the tomato, the bean, potato, sweet peppers and maize. These vegetables did not automatically become the favourites that they are today; it took at least two more centuries for people to acquaint themselves with these newcomers.

Oranges too were introduced by the Portuguese

during the 15th century, as the root of the name in a number of languages – *portugallo* – indicates.

Modern additions of vegetables and fruit, such as avocado, cultivated mushrooms or kiwi fruit, have not been assimilated into the culinary culture and are grown mainly for export purposes.

One can appreciate the character of Mediterranean food as an entity not only by the similarities of the ingredients but also by the fashion in which they are used, that is the cooking. People in the 15th century could move from one country to another and still find the same climate and the same dishes on the table and so feel at home. This, to a large extent, remains true today.

THE HEALTHIEST OF FOODS

T he Mediterranean landscape is dominated by the large expanse of blue at its centre, 970,000 square miles of it. Inland, the terrain is hilly, rocky and arid and the lack of pasture is obvious. The result: scarcity of cows and consequently of rich dairy produce. The small landholdings have to be laboriously terraced before they are cultivated or planted with trees.

The climate, balmy and sunny, pampers and uplifts the human soul but its aridity scorches the land. The result: small-scale agriculture, garden-based. None of the vast expanses of grain so familiar in Northern countries will be found here.

Nevertheless winter cannot be relied upon as a clement friend and provision has to be made, the larders must be filled. Because of the small-scale, garden-based agriculture and the lack of grain, the Mediterranean peasant picked and dried his vegetables and stored them, usually under his wooden bed with its special compartments, like the most valuable commodity that they were, so there would not be hunger in the winter, if winter was to be foe.

THE HAPPY MARRIAGE OF PULSES AND OLIVE OIL

Beans of all colours and sizes, lentils, peas, broad beans and chickpeas have been the staples of Mediterranean societies since ancient times, as was bread; although grain often had to be imported from other countries in exchange for the typical Mediterranean produce, olive oil and wine.

Pulses, probably the richest source of protein other than meat, and with a high fibre content (both automatically associated with healthy eating), were dried in the sun and stored. With these and his beautifully-shaped, pregnant earthenware pots full of that liquid commodity from the trees, the olive oil, the Mediterranean peasant was secure and his food was the result of marrying one to the other, a natural outcome of such an approximation. As olive oil contains mono-unsaturated fatty acids, it is one of the healthiest cooking mediums, which is proved by the long-lived peasantry of village communities who rely upon it.

Rice, pasta, bread and the North African *couscous* – all grain-based foods – have with pulses formed the staples of Mediterranean cooking and have meant survival to the poor. They helped to build up a cuisine among the healthiest in the world!

MEAT AND DAIRY PRODUCE

The lack of pastures in the area has limited the animals that could be raised. Cows, bred in limited numbers, have to be kept indoors in the hot and dry weather and are expensive to feed; therefore they constitute a luxury. They are mostly reared and kept in the North, away from the hot Mediterranean zone.

Instead, light and strong-footed sheep and goats are the royals of the kingdom; but these have always been most treasured by peasant communities for their milk so yoghourt and cheese can be made in order to enliven the vegetable and pulse-orientated table. Meat has been a luxury kept for celebrations and religious occasions: the baptism of a son, the marrying of a daughter, Easter, or an engagement. And so it was to be dispensable in Mediterranean cuisine, which even today is based on ingredients other than meat. As a result, the lack of butter was not missed, for it was an alien commodity, looked down upon by the ancients as the food of barbarians. And even nowadays when they talk of butter in the Mediterranean, they mostly mean margarine.

SEAFOOD IN MEDITERRANEAN CUISINE

But of course there was always the sea and those who had access to it livened up their tables with its treasures. Glistening fish of all hues found their way into the Mediterranean kitchen or garden (as a lot of the cooking is done on charcoal, in the open air). Octopus hangs in the sun to dry and becomes part of the main culinary themes of the area: the *mezze*. Squid and cuttlefish adorn dishes with their wicked, ebonied darkness, their ink; or they are cooked whole on charcoal and served in wonderful dishes such as the Spanish *Parillada*, a collection of the freshest of seafoods served on a huge plate.

The array of seafood in a Mediterranean market is exotic enough to seem almost an oddity and certainly an indulgence to the uninitiated Northerner's eyes. Visiting a large market, such as the San José Market off the Ramblas in beautiful Barcelona, is a cultural experience, not simply a gastronomic one. Mussels, clams of all sizes and hues, sea-snails, bizarre, heavily clawed *percebes*, oysters, razor shells, shrimps and prawns of all sizes, scallops, mingle with the opaque sides of salted cod in the next stall. When fish is not eaten fresh, it is eaten salted. It is soaked and dressed in olive oil before finding itself defiantly on the table, boosting the more acquiescent vegetable dishes.

The favourite method of cooking fish is on open fires and this is where any respectable-sized and bright-eyed specimen, sprinkled with mountain herbs and a little olive oil, will find itself.

All in all, fish is only second to vegetables and pulses in the culinary race.

VEGETABLES AND FRUIT

Above all the cuisine follows the seasons. The rhythm of the climate is obeyed and the result, even nowadays, is seasonal. Vegetables such as peas, globe artichokes and salad greens prefer the mellow spring; others such as courgettes, aubergines and beans, the heat of the summer in varying degrees;

and the same applies to fruit. Harvests are gathered at the optimum moment; a moment which is also optimum for the kitchen but certainly not for the freezer or the canning industry. Freshness accounts for most of the charm of the cuisine and frozen or par-boiled canned specimens have no part in it.

Luscious fruits, luxuriously piled, exhibiting their sparkling colours and shapes, are a temptation to the eye. It is fruit and not rich puddings that finishes a Mediterranean meal. Fruit is also eaten unceremoniously throughout the day, often squeezed into wonderful drinks, made into mouth-watering ice-creams, spoon preserves, crystallised morsels, and used in casseroles with meat.

The presence of all kinds of nuts is also evident in Mediterranean cuisine; walnuts, hazelnuts, chestnuts, pistachios, pine kernels and roasted seeds from various fruits are part of everyday life.

These are the ingredients of the culinary culture which have developed largely because of the climate and the terrain. They have made Mediterranean cuisine one of the healthiest in the world.

THE DISHES AND THEIR CONTINUITY

The food of the poor, the simple food, survives time and perpetuates itself through the centuries. Various examples can be found around the Mediterranean basin. One such dish is the Italian *Spinaci alla Romana* which contains raisins and pine nuts. Similar recipes are also found in Catalonia in Spain and in North Africa, sometimes with fried courgettes instead. This variation was assumed to be of Arab influence, but Apicius (*Apicius de Re Quoquinaria*, probably compiled by an editor in the 4th or 5th century and not the Roman Apicius himself) mentions a very similar dish with courgettes and pine nuts, the latter being quite popular in the ancient world. Where was the influence from? The colonising Greeks? The colonising Arabs? Or did the Roman legionnaires stumble across it at some eastern source?

GARLIC SAUCES

The ancient Greeks, being fond of garlic, concocted a sharp sauce made with pulped garlic and olive oil which they called *Skorothalmi*, a particular favourite of Ancient Athenians. This is none other than the modern Greek *Skorthalia*, which has come down through the ages and which is served with boiled or fried vegetables or fish, and in particular salted fish as in Spain and Italy. Diluted with water it makes the cool Andalusian soup *Gazpacho Blanco*.

Offshoots of this sauce can be found along most Mediterranean coasts, with minor variations. There is *Aioli* in France, a grand version of which is the traditional supper on Christmas Eve. There is *Agliata* in Italy, *Tarator* in Turkey and the Middle East, and in Spain *All-i-Oli*. From there to *Mayonnaise*, it was only a small step. The garlic was dropped and the thickening agent was egg yolks, as in the French *Aioli*, instead of bread and walnuts or almonds as in all other versions.

GRAIN-BASED DISHES

The North African subsistence dishes of *Couscous*, and the Sicilian *Cuscusu* which is only eaten with fish, are probably related to Italian *Polenta*. All are grain-based dishes cooked in steam, though polenta nowadays is made with maize flour. Polenta, in its turn, is a close relative of the Roman *Pulmentum*.

FISH

Even if the vegetation of the Mediterranean was different originally, the sea was much the same (less polluted and exploited), and the fish exactly the same if more plentiful. The sea has always been a major source of food, and fish was the subject of detailed diatribes by Aristotle and Archistratos. Delicious fish soups are to be found all over the Mediterranean. Dioscorides praised their qualities and suggested that they should be made with rock fish such as the ferocious-looking pink scorpions, *Rascasse Rouge*, '. . . sod with nothing else but water and oyle and Annise'.

Supposedly, the Greek fishermen's soup *Kakavia* derives its name from the pot it was cooked in, the *kakavi*, and there are mentions of it in Aristophanes. The French *Bouillabaisse* bears a great many similarities to *Kakavia* and it may have been introduced to Marseilles by the colonising Phocaeans.

This kind of fish soup is similar to the Italian *Brodetti* and the French *Soupe de Poissons*.

'Agamemnon and Achilles are supposed to have eaten it under the walls of Troy, and in comparatively modern times Julius Caesar downed a bowl of it before crossing the Rubicon. Dante ate it in exile at Porto Corsino, Napoleon fortified himself with it before escaping from Elba, and Field Marshal Montgomery celebrated victory with *brodetti* at almost the same spot where Caesar indulged in it.'

Waverley Root in his *Italian Food*, 1974

OLIVES

Olives are universal around the Mediterranean. Not only are they eaten at all times of day and put into salads, such as the Greek *Horiatiki* and the French *Niçoise*, but they are cooked with all kinds of game (*Perthikes me Elies*, the Greek casserole of partridges with olives), poultry (the Moroccan *Djej bil Zeetoon* and the Greek, *Kotopoulo me Elies*), and meat (the Greek *Soutzoukakia Smyrneika*, originating in Smyrna, the Andalusian *Carne Machada à la Andalusa* and the French casserole of beef called *La Daube*).

They are also embedded in Italian *Pizza*, the Provençal *Pissaladière*, and in the sauce of *Spaghetti alla Puttanesca*. They are mashed for the sharp Provençal spread *Tapenade*, and they are cooked with fish as in the Andalusian *Bonito con Aceitunas*, made from fresh tuna with green olives. In Greece and France, black olives are added to baked salted cod.

Finally in their most exquisite form, olives are one of the main ingredients of the sharply appetising Greek-Cypriot bread, *Eliopsomo*.

BEANS

And, of course, there are beans, beans and more beans! Beans of all shapes, sizes and hues; creamy haricot or cannellini beans; beautifully striped scarlet *borlotti*; the flat large butter bean types which are called *schiaccioni* in Italy, *gigantes* (giants) in Greece and 'elephants' elsewhere, the eccentric black-eyed beans, the dark tanned broad beans, and many more. And there are lentils and chickpeas, deliciously transformed into casseroles, thick soups, rissoles, salads and dips.

Those who are accustomed to a summer Mediterranean table, and alas only that of a restaurant, won't have realised the importance of these humble and shy occupants of the kitchen shelf, particularly on the eastern shores. Plebeians they may be in other cultures, but in the Mediterranean they are royalty!

RECIPES

BAGNA CAUDA

GARLIC AND ANCHOVY DIP (ITALY)

A robust, peasant dish from the Piedmont area of the North of Italy which plays tremendous tricks on your appetite! Serve it as you would a *fondue*, but if you do not have the special set simply use a small saucepan. Anchovies are sold salted out of large barrels or tins all over the Mediterranean, but here I have had to substitute drained anchovies in oil. Serve a platter of trimmed, washed and quartered vegetables, such as celery, firm courgettes, cauliflower, sweet peppers, and young artichokes, to be dipped in communally. Offer crusty fresh bread as well.

3 cloves garlic, *finely sliced*
5 tablespoons olive oil
6 drained anchovies, *chopped*
1 oz (30 g) butter
Black pepper

Sauté the garlic in the hot oil without allowing it to turn brown. Add the anchovies, some black pepper and cook slowly for 10 minutes, stirring occasionally, until thickened. Add the butter, stir for 1–2 minutes until well amalgamated and take to the table.

Serves 4–6

SOUPE DE POISSONS

FISH SOUP (FRANCE/PROVENCE)

Although it is difficult to make an authentic Mediterranean fish soup in this country, good alternatives can be improvised. (But I must hastily add that fish soup, unless eaten in the open air within reach of the sea, will never invoke the same taste or charm!) However, do not despair!

2 lb (1 kg) fish (monkfish, halibut or whiting fillets)
1 large onion, sliced
2 cloves garlic, sliced
5 tablespoons olive oil
1 small Florentine fennel, trimmed and chopped
3 medium tomatoes, peeled and chopped
1 glass white wine
2 pints (1.1 l) fish stock made with heads and bones
½ teaspoon dried thyme
Large pinch saffron, soaked in hot water for 10 minutes
Salt and cayenne pepper

Skin fish and take out obvious bones, if any. Wash and slice it.

Sauté the onion and garlic in hot oil. Add the fennel and continue to sauté a little longer. Add the tomatoes, wine, fish stock, herbs and seasoning. Bring to the boil, add the fish, cover and cook briskly for 15 minutes.

Liquidise into a coarse purée. Heat, adjust seasoning and serve with fried croûtons, or pour over toasted strips of bread which have been rubbed with garlic.

Serves 6

SPAGHETTI ALLA PUTTANESCA (ITALY)

The origin of this memorable dish is surrounded by rumours. One of them has it that unfaithful Neapolitan wives, having spent their afternoons in illicit circumstances, returned home late and quickly prepared this undemanding dish. Well, try it – at least the dish!

2 cloves garlic, finely sliced
6–8 anchovy fillets, chopped
4 tablespoons olive oil
4 oz (110 g) black olives, pitted and halved
1 tablespoon capers
1 small dried chilli, de-seeded
1 lb (450 g) tomatoes, peeled and chopped or
    14 oz (396 g) tin of tomatoes, finely chopped
Salt
8 oz (225 g) spaghetti

First make the sauce. Sauté the garlic and anchovies in the hot oil until aromatic, then add olives, capers and chilli and fry for a few more seconds. Add the tomatoes and salt, cover and cook gently for 15–20 minutes until the sauce has thickened.

Boil the spaghetti in plenty of salted boiling water for about 8 minutes, without overcooking. Strain, mix with the sauce, toss and serve immediately.

Serves 3–4

KESKSOU

COUSCOUS (NORTH AFRICA)

In Tunisia, Morocco and Algeria couscous, made from semolina and coated with flour in order to keep the grains separate, is the national dish. Each family used to make their own couscous but nowadays it is mostly made from ready-made grains which are easily obtainable in this country too.

Dexterous handling of the grains is vital to the lightness of the finished dish, which should on no account be lumpy and stodgy. Moreover the grains must cook in steam and never touch the water or broth underneath. For this purpose a special container called a *couscousière* is used. This consists of two parts: the lower, which is a large saucepan where the stew to be served with the grains is cooked; the upper has a finely perforated base, where the grains are placed. Originally these were made of earthenware as were many cooking, eating and drinking utensils; nowadays they are made from aluminium and they can be found in specialist shops. Alternatively one can improvise by fitting a colander on top of a saucepan (line the colander with cheesecloth or an old cotton kitchen towel if its holes are wider than the grain).

The main principle is to wet and fluff the grains up and be patient at the same time; it needs about 40 minutes to cook and 20 minutes to rest.

6 oz (175 g) couscous
½ pt (300 ml) water
1 tablespoon oil
Salt

First spread the grains and gradually sprinkle on the cold water and a tablespoon of oil, working it in gently with your fingers. Let it rest and swell for 15 minutes, working it through the tips of the fingers occasionally to break any lumps. Place the grains on the steamer without covering and steam for 20 minutes. Spread it in a shallow container again, sprinkle with a little more water and salt and work it through your fingers, spreading it evenly and allowing it to dry out for 15 minutes. If it has to wait at this stage cover it with a damp cloth. Put it back into the steamer and steam for 20 more minutes; the steaming can be done over boiling water if you have prepared a casserole separately. Serve it with the *Date Tagine* (page 55), or you can improvise spicy casseroles of chicken, vegetables and chickpeas.

Serves 4–6

LOUVIA ME SPANAKI

BEAN AND SPINACH CASSEROLE
(CYPRUS)

Among beans, it is the black-eyed one that bears the most unmistakable earthy flavours, unpolished but enticing, with a unique texture to match its other qualities. These beans do not need soaking and only need about 30 minutes to cook. They are most popular in Cyprus and the Middle East, where combined with fresh vegetables such as spinach or courgettes they make substantial casseroles.

This dish, which is accentuated with the aromatic addition of the fried garlic – probably reminiscent of an Arab tradition – can be served as a main course with sharp olives, fried squid or as a substantial salad.

8 oz (225 g) black-eyed beans, picked clean and washed
1 lb (450 g) fresh spinach or a 10 oz (285 g) packet
*   frozen spinach*
3 tablespoons lemon juice
6 tablespoons olive oil
2 cloves garlic, peeled and crushed
1 teaspoon cummin powder
Salt and black pepper

Cover beans with water, boil for 4 minutes and strain. Cover with fresh water, add the lemon juice (which will safeguard against the inky hue they normally acquire), cover and cook for 20 minutes.

In the meantime, wash thoroughly, strain and roughly chop the fresh spinach, or allow the frozen packet spinach to defrost. Add spinach and seasoning to the beans and cook for 10 more minutes, or slightly less if frozen. Sauté the garlic in the hot oil in a frying pan, without browning it, then add the cummin, stir together for 1–2 minutes until aromatic and pour over beans. Mix well and serve. It can also be served at room temperature.

Serves 4

THE UBIQUITOUS OLIVE

Olive trees were created, according to myth, out of an antagonistic moment between two Greek gods – Poseidon, menacing-looking god of the sea, and Athena, goddess of wisdom and learning – over the patronage of the city of Athens. Athena won with her creation, the olive tree, symbol of peace and victory, and so she became the patron goddess of the city which was named after her.

The Greeks seem to have exported both olive trees and olive oil eastwards as well as westwards. The olive trees in Provence, for instance, are reputed to have been planted by the colonising Greeks 2,500 years ago, and rumour has it that even today there are some trees surviving from that distant past.

The most convincing piece of evidence for the presence of the olive tree in the Eastern Mediterranean is that olive leaves and branches were found in all three wreaths inside the coffins of Tutankhamen, by Howard Carter and Lord Carnarvon in 1922.

Trees start to bear fruit in the fifth or sixth year of their life and because of the shortage of water they bear fruit biennially. It takes five kilos of olives to produce one kilo of the golden liquid, the olive oil.

Harvesting the olives is a winter job and in a uniquely biblical way it is still mainly a family task.

Green Olives
Olives are picked at various stages and for various purposes. First the green unripe olives are selected quite early, towards the end of August or early September. They are cracked and dropped in brine, and as they are the mildest among olives, they take their flavours from the aromatics added to the brine, such as coriander seeds, garlic and origanum.

Dark Olives
Next, the olives are harvested as they turn purple or black. These are also for table use and they are pre-

pared by either going into brine or packed with layers of coarse salt and a weight on top.

Black Olives
Lastly, in late October, the indiscriminate olive picking starts, aimed at ripe olives. Sheets of plastic or hessian are spread underneath each tree, the earth having been cleared of weeds and hoed beforehand. The olive branches are hit with log cypress sticks and the fruit is gathered underneath. Higher branches are reached by ladders and the trees are pruned at the same time.

Olive oil
The olive presses, now mechanised, until quite recently used to be operated manually with the help of a mule or a horse. Hot water is mostly used for pressing the whole olives into a pulp. The extracted oil mixed with the water is then automatically drained out into a tank where the oil rises to the top and is then filtered off and re-directed into special containers. 'And the floors shall be full of wheat, and the fats (vats) shall overflow with wine and oil,' says Joel II, 24.

The best olive oil is the one with the least acidity. This is referred to as *virgin* and it is the first extract from the olives. This is the purest and the most aromatic, the one that bears closest similarities to the fruit. A second pressing of husks, stones, *et al* brings inferior results.

The texture of the best olive oil is thick and velvety and it has a greenish hue, with a predominant taste of the fruit embodied in it. The oil from Tuscany is considered to be the most superior. People who prefer a milder taste should opt for the more refined oils with a blander taste and a mellow golden colour.

Other Uses of Olive Oil
* Olive oil is taken to relieve constipation.
* A piece of cotton wool drenched in warmed olive oil is inserted in the affected ear to cure earache.
* Warm olive oil is rubbed on ailing parts such as sprained ankles.
* It is rubbed on the skull to prevent dandruff.
* Mixed with vinegar, olive oil clears up hair infestation.
* Olive oil features in most religious ceremonies, from baptisms to extreme unction, and in rituals to dispel the evil eye.
* Most importantly, it used to fill the lamps of the poor peasants to give them light.
* Olive oil is so intertwined in Mediterranean culture that it is not surprising that it has been attributed aphrodisiac qualities. *'Fae lathi k'ela vrathi'* – Eat olive oil if you are to come and spend the night, says the Greek proverb suggestively.

COOKING METHODS

M ethods is an inappropriate word to use in the
Mediterranean context, unsuited to the spirit
and the *status quo* of the area. Few are the instances
that can be assigned the honour of the adjective
methodical! The fashion in which food is cooked,
even at present times, would, to say the least, seem
eccentric to the Westerner, almost touching on the
folkloric.

If one were to take a stroll on a brilliant, sunlit
Sunday morning in a residential area in a large city
such as Athens or Istanbul or on a large island such
as Malta or Cyprus or even a small island such as
Skopelos or Sifnos in the Aegean, one would
encounter the charming spectacle of people (black-
clad old ladies, if you were lucky) carrying large aluminium baking dishes filled with all sorts of
colourful delights and exuding raw garlic and fragrant herby aromas. A small goat leg surrounded by
quartered potatoes, a chicken surrounded with
exotic *okra*, the multinational assemblage of stuffed
vegetables with their bright green, scarlet and fiery
mauve intermingled, the pies, the pasta, etc. These
dishes and many more are taken to the local bakers
daily, where they are cooked along with the bread in
cavernous, nowadays mostly electrical, ovens for a
ludicrously small fee. Ingenious and economical!

Names or numbers are scribbled on the container,
and come lunchtime the festive sight of a colourful
assembly awaiting collection is, for me, one of the

most exhilarating spectacles, both visually as well as aromatically! Along with visits to local archaeological sites, make sure of a visit to the local baker's if you want to engulf yourself in local colour and emerge more knowledgeable and understanding of things Mediterranean.

Cooking has been done on home hearths, primus stoves or on bottled gas stoves, and the lack of ovens in the home brought in the use of the local baker; and so it continues to the present day. We all take advantage of the poor baker, including of course myself, when I am in Greece. (He can also be blamed for culinary disasters – too much salt, too much water, dishes overcooked or burned.)

Beehive-shaped ovens are to be seen in peasant household yards in Greece, Turkey, Sicily, Sardinia

and Morocco. These are fired with small sticks of wood which, once the oven is fiery hot, are drawn out and kept at its entrance while the food goes in. They are very effective as food needs shorter time to cook and tastes indeed different. (We have such an outdoor oven in Greece, which is reputed to bake the best bread in the village.)

Home hearths have inspired the long simmering of foods in traditional dishes, such as the North African *Tagines* and *Couscous*, or the Spanish *Cocidos*. The common use of pulses, particularly in Greece, Turkey, Egypt and Spain, also favours this method of cooking and adapts well to it.

THE AROMATICS

I f one were to form a sweeping impression of the aroma engulfing a Mediterranean kitchen, the first sensation would overwhelmingly be that of the fragrant hills. It is from these stony hills and from under the olive and the fig trees that people have found their inspiration for enhancing their dishes.

It is the sweet, summery aroma of the purple-flowering thyme bushes on rocky ground, as they are heat loving plants; the pungency of the creamy flowers of the woody stalks of the wild origano under the gnarled fig trees, as they are moisture seekers. It is the brilliant green feathers of aristocratic, slender dill, in spring, and its seeds at the height of the summer. It is the musky aroma of wild sage in early summer. There are glossy bay leaves, the sharp, dark needles of the rosemary, and the minute silky leaves of the wild mint, most refreshingly scented.

There is also parsley used in profusion, chervil and fresh coriander.

These and many more, regionally characteristic, are the aromas of the Mediterranean kitchen, often coupled with the fragrance of the Orient – the exotic immigrants to the region, the spices.

PICKING WILD HERBS

The optimum time for picking herbs is at the height of their life; that is, at their most aromatic. (Before embarking on herb picking, ask the locals for the favourite spots of each species.)

Thyme and origano should be flowering when they are picked, so the middle of July onwards is the best time. Small bunches of both flowers and leaves should be hung in the sun for four days until dry, then crumbled into storage jars and the stalks discarded. It is these jars that will bring summer into your kitchen in the gloomiest of days and fill your eyes with evocative pictures.

Mint flowers a little earlier, in late May and early June; it should be handled gently as it is fragile and crumbles easily.

Sage branches, at their best around late June, can be made into bunches, dried in the sun and then hung in the kitchen for use throughout the winter.

And of course there is the world of *tisanes* – exquisite infusions made from wild-growing herbs that would need a small book in their own right. Camomile, verbena, sage, lime, mint and thyme are the most familiar, but the list is endless and each village community has its own favourites. Tisanes are popular from Turkey in the East to Spain in the West.

Enchanting stores specialising in wild herbs – not only for culinary purposes but also for medicinal uses, aphrodisiac potions, beauty preparations and magic potions against the '*evil eye*' – are to be found in the vicinity of most traditional Mediterranean markets and they are worth visiting. The most fascinating are to be found in Morocco, Turkey, Greece and Egypt.

RECIPES

PESTO

BASIL SAUCE (ITALY)

Italy is the land where round heads of basil grow out of whitewashed pots, with the sweetest of scents. Serve spaghetti with pesto sauce, perfect for an *al fresco* meal under a vine.

1 full teacup basil leaves
2 cloves garlic, peeled and chopped
2 tablespoons pine kernels
2 tablespoons grated Parmesan and Sardinian Pecorino cheese
3 tablespoons good olive oil
Salt

Place all the ingredients in a blender, add a few drops of water and blend until creamy. Warm in a small saucepan, but without allowing it to come to the boil. Mix with spaghetti which has been cooked *al dente*, toss gently and serve immediately.

CACIK

YOGHOURT AND CUCUMBER SALAD
(TURKEY)

One of the most refreshing appetisers to be found in the Eastern Mediterranean. Serve it with fried vegetables such as courgettes and aubergines, or on its own with bread and some black olives as *mezze*. It can also be served with roast chicken or lamb.

1 tablespoon olive oil
1 teaspoon wine vinegar
1 clove garlic, peeled and crushed
5 oz (150 g) carton plain yoghourt
2 in (5 cm) cucumber, peeled and diced finely or coarsely grated
Salt
2–3 sprigs fresh mint, finely chopped, or ½ teaspoon dried mint

Combine oil, vinegar and garlic in a bowl and beat a little with a fork. Add yoghourt and beat until creamy and well amalgamated. Add cucumber, salt and the mint and mix well. Serve chilled.

Serves 4

AFELIA

PORK IN RED WINE (CYPRUS)

A spicy casserole among the best known dishes from the island of Cyprus and very popular among Cypriot families. Serve with fried potatoes or rice and a salad.

2 tablespoons coriander seeds, crushed thickly
2 lb (1 kg) boned lean pork such as tenderloin, cubed
1 glass red wine
1/2 teaspoon black peppercorns, crushed thickly
2 sticks cinnamon
Salt
5 tablespoons vegetable oil

Pick the coriander clean from stones first. Wipe and marinate meat in the wine and spices overnight. Brown the meat in hot oil until crisp, then add the marinade, cover and cook for 20 minutes until the liquid has evaporated and a smooth sauce remains.

Serves 4–6

THE DRINKS

W ine is the drink most closely associated with the Mediterranean. It was here that the wild vines were pruned and tended and fermented grape juice was polished and transformed into the smooth, satisfying wines of present day.

The Greeks originally developed wine-making, producing it commercially during the Mycenean civilisation and exporting it for centuries after. Wine was so important to the Greeks that they even assigned a god to it, Dionysus. Special festivities were held in his honour, attended by people garlanded with wild flowers. They also introduced viniculture to their colonies and are reputed to have brought it as far as Marseilles along with the olive tree. They, later, taught the Romans the secrets of wine-making.

It has been a universal custom across the Mediterranean to offer jugs of wine with thickly sliced fruit in it. Apples and oranges, pears, luscious peaches and nectarines are the familiar ones. In Spain, the most common drink in every workers' *bodega* is a jug of *Sangria*. This is red wine mixed with soda water or lemonade and unpeeled slices of oranges and lemons.

Beer was made by the Ancient Egyptians and has been popular ever since, despite the rather exaggerated warning of the Greek writer Dioscorides from Cilicia that 'it hurts the kidneys and nerves, bad for the Meninges [Brain], it causes wind, bad humour and Leprosie'.

Further distillations from grape skins that are left after being pressed for wine-making produce drinks such as the Greek *Tsipouro*, Turkish *Raki* and the Middle Eastern *Arak*. These drinks are sometimes flavoured with aniseed, like the Spanish *Anis* and the Greek *Ouzo* which are diluted with cold water to produce an opaque-cloudy long refreshing drink, or the French *Pernod*, which can be diluted with water, lemonade or even orange juice. On the island of Chios, in Greece, the same drink is flavoured with the aromatic resin of the mastic tree and it is appropriately called *Mastiha*. Mastiha, as the hard resin is also called, was what children chewed before bubble gum was imported from the United States.

The North Africans are non-alcohol drinkers, faithful to the *Koran*. Their universal drink is sweetened (sometimes excessively) mint tea. The more highly flavoured and aromatic the variety of mint, the more sought after it becomes. Mint tea is automatically offered to the visitor as a sign of hospitality in the same way that small cups of Turkish coffee, accompanied by a glass of cold water, are offered in countries all over the Eastern Mediterranean.

Non-alcoholic *sherbets* are made from fruit such as sour cherries, almonds, oranges, and so on. And in Turkey, where yoghourt has been a staple food at all times, they also make a drink with it called *Ayran*, as they do in the Lebanon and Syria where it is called *Laban*.

RECIPE

SANGRIA (SPAIN)

Sangria is the drink most commonly served in every dark and smoky *bodega* in Spain. Poured from terracotta jugs it is extremely refreshing, despite its alcoholic content. It is best made the day before in order to allow the fruit to macerate and add its aromas to the wine. Brandy can be added, but is usually omitted in Spain. Soda water can be used instead of lemonade, if you prefer. Often Spanish families add 1–2 sticks of cinnamon as the general belief is that the drink then 'goes quicker to your head'.

1 bottle red wine
1 tablespoon sugar
1 orange, washed and sliced in circles
1 lemon, washed and sliced in circles
1 cinnamon stick
1 teacup lemonade

Mix all the ingredients apart from the lemonade in a jug and refrigerate for a few hours or overnight. Add the lemonade and some ice just before it is to be served. Serve, allowing some fruit in each glass.

THE EVIL EYE

M editerraneans are on the whole extremely superstitious, the main anxiety being the notorious *evil eye*. For instance, on exclaiming how fast a child runs, he or she instantly ends up on the ground with knees grazed; or if expressing admiration for the beautiful frock a little girl is wearing, she immediately falls into a pool of mud. Such remarks 'tempt fate'. The admirer is then accused of having an *evil eye*, the undertones of which imply hidden envy in the first place. From there on, the person in question becomes quite undesirable and is treated with suspicion.

The evil eye may also cause illnesses such as headache, nausea and fainting. To counteract it, there are various remedies, most of them containing garlic in some form or other. In Greece, a prophylactic measure is to recite immediately at a hint of danger '*Skortha sta matia sou*' – Garlic in your eyes – which is believed to dispel the power of evil. (My grandmother was endlessly reciting this line.)

Other more permanent measures, which occur all over the Eastern Mediterranean, are for cloves of garlic to be sewn in the lining of garments worn by adults, children or babies who may tempt or provoke the evil eye. Such people are regarded as being beautiful, extremely intelligent or simply charming. (As most parents think their children fit one of the above categories, inevitably garlic figures largely in every family's life and garments.)

In Egypt, an even more complicated procedure is

described by Lane in his *Manners and Customs of the Modern Egyptians*, published in 1898.

Allum is very generally used in the following manner by the people of Egypt, to counteract the effects of the evil eye. A piece of about the size of a walnut is placed upon burning coals and left until it has ceased to bubble. This should be done a short time before sunset; and the person who performs the operation should repeat three times, while the allum is burning, the first chapter of the Kur-an and the last three chapters of the same, all of which are very short. On taking the allum off the fire, it will be found (we are told) to have assumed the form of the person whose envy or malice has given occasion for this process; it is then pounded, put into some food and given to a black dog to be eaten.

If, however, the evil eye has not been prevented, perhaps by negligence, and has already cast its devilish shadows on somebody (human or beast) who displays signs of lethargy, nausea or severe headache, then it has to be exorcised by a woman in one of various ways. One such method in either Greece or Turkey is to have a glass full of water with some olive oil on top; a clove inserted on top of a needle, is then set alight, and while the name of one of the suspects is recited the burning clove is plunged into the olive oil and as it is extinguished it cracks and spatters. One clove after another is burnt, until all the suspects are exhausted and the clove that creates the most riotous effect is the one depicting the maligning person. Once he or she is uncovered, the sufferer starts to be relieved from the symptoms.

Although these exorcisms are expiated by women, the secret words of each one – a family secret probably – can only be communicated to another woman through a man and in complete secrecy.

Other manifestations of the evil eye appear in replicas of glass beads almost all over the Mediterranean. They are displayed in prominent positions in order to attract and so avert the evil eye. These blue-coloured beads are often hung not only on humans but also around the collar of animals, donkeys, mules or goats; also on boats, cars, lorries or whatever possessions are treasured most in a Mediterranean household. On the island of Malta, a large, brightly-coloured eye is depicted on either side of a boat's prow.

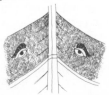

In the south of Spain, *mal de ojo* – evil eye – is averted by wearing amulets of the Madonna which are joined by a pearl for little girls. Also, the word *serpiente* – serpent – is taboo as it is believed to attract the evil eye: a form of religious superstition absorbed into popular culture and manifesting itself in a non-religious context, but nevertheless clearly connected with Eve and the primeval sin in the Garden of Eden.

These are the most prominent superstitions, but there are many more. Many can be traced back to ancient, pre-Christian myths and rituals, especially those connected with the seasons and with the planting and harvesting of crops. In the Eastern Mediterranean, the foundations of a new building have to be moistened with the blood of a cockerel, which is then boiled and fed to the labourers, – an ancient allegory of strength and robustness associated with blood as well as manhood.

MEDITERRANEAN FESTIVITIES

'On the same night, too [New Year's Eve], takes place the ceremony of cutting "St Basil's cake" – a large circular mass of *brioche* with almonds and walnuts upon it, which is solemnly cut open, shortly before midnight, by the head of the house. Sometimes a franc or a gold piece is put into the cake, and the person receiving the piece which contains the coin is supposed to be going to have a lucky year.'

Greek Life in Town and Country,
William Miller, London, 1905

This ritual is still enacted in exactly the same way in Greece. At the same hour, in Spain, people tune to the Porta del Sol clock in Madrid through their radios or televisions in order to hear the clock strike midnight; with each stroke everyone has to consume a grape, and by the twelfth stroke twelve grapes must have been eaten, otherwise it is considered an ill omen for the New Year.

In France, particularly in Provence, Christmas Eve is celebrated traditionally with the most ritualistic meal of the whole year, *Le Grand Aïoli*. This consists of strictly Lenten food. Fish, mostly boiled, such as salted cod, octopus, sea snails and squid, and *petit gris* snails and boiled vegetables, such as artichokes, potatoes, carrots, cauliflower, asparagus, green beans and chickpeas and eggs are among the prime items of the celebratory table. But the *grand* place belongs, indisputably, to the *Aïoli* – the smooth, thick, garlic mayonnaise made with the exquisite *virgin* Provençal olive oil. The desserts that follow should, according to the ritual, be thirteen. The number is made up by bowls of dried and fresh fruits, nuts, exquisite nougats, perhaps a baked tart, and always *pompe à l'huile*, a dry biscuit made with olive oil.

Fish is also the Christmas Eve supper in Italy, while in Andalusia they start with a sweet almond soup – *Sopa de Almendras*. A splendid array of traditional sweets, the Spanish *Turrones* or Italian *Torrone* – variations of nougat – which are made with quantities of almonds, honey, and eggs, characterise Christmas in both countries. In Spain, there are *Pasteles de Gloria* from Alicante, *Turron de Alicante*, the familiar hard nougat, or *Turron de Jijona*, a soft and sensuously honeyed version, the walnut-shaped, pine-studded *Pinonates*, *Figuritas de Mazapan* from romantic Toledo, and many more.

In Greece, every family makes huge quantities of almond-based *Kourabiethes* and dark, honeyed *Phinikia*.

Mediterranean feasts are distinctive and colourful. Their roots lie in pre-Christian origins associated with the seasons and the crops, and often it is impossible to disentangle paganism from Christianity. Feasts are preceded by a *cathartic* period, which is meant to be both spiritual as well as physical.

The major Mediterranean festival is Easter, clearly associated with spring and the re-awakening of life in nature. During the 40-day period of Lent people abstain from meat and most animal produce. Instead, quantities of fish and all kinds of seafood are consumed, with Fridays solely devoted to various dishes of salted cod which has been a staple food since the Middle Ages. Such dishes figure on every respectable restaurant's menu on Lenten Fridays; from fashionable restaurants in Rome or cosmopolitan Florence to bustling ports like Piraeus, Barcelona and Marseilles.

In Greece, the first day of Lent is appropriately called *Kathari Theftera* – Clean Monday – during which people have picnics in the open air and devour quantities of olives, spring onions, sea food, raw vegetables, *Taramosalata* and special bread, the *Lagana*.

Holy Week is studded with rituals and permeated with mystique. The passionate expressions of mystical fear spill from churches into the streets, where many colourful processions take place. In Spain, and particularly in Andalucia, these are extraordinarily expressive! Superbly painted and elaborately dressed, statues of the Virgin are carried through the streets, often preceded by awe-inspiring, long-hooded, brown-cloaked figures, against the background of the murmuring, singing and lamenting women, until the spring air becomes resonant with grief and at the same time hope. Similarly ritualistic processions take place in Italy, while in Malta and Greece they have a more subdued, mystical character, with silent followers holding lit candles, accompanied by soft Byzantine chanting.

On Easter Sunday, the religious climax coincides with the universal sacrificial ritual of the young spring lambs that figure on the menu of most countries. Hard-boiled eggs are coloured and superbly decorated for the occasion.

Ramadan is perhaps the major Islamic event, commemorating the time that the Prophet withdrew to desert solitude, praying and fasting. During

Ramadan, the faithful Muslims observe a similar absolute fast which permits neither food nor water during the daytime. It is believed that fasting during Ramadan expiates one's sins, and during this holy month the gates of Heaven remain open, while those of hell are closed with the devils chained up within.

In North Africa the firing of a cannon at the end of each day is the signal for the meal to start. People break their fast in the evening with *Harira*, a soup made with chicken or meat broth, vegetables, chickpeas or lentils, and fragrant with fresh coriander and parsley. This is traditionally served with dates or figs. *Hariras* may be sampled in the unpretentious establishments of Fez and Marakesh. The arrival of the evening, apart from the end of the fasting, also signals the beginning of all kinds of street festivities. Men gather in coffee shops, where they are entertained by wandering bards of the Homeric tradition, chanting traditional songs and reciting legendary poems to the accompaniment of a special instrument, a single-string fiddle, the *Rebab*.

The end of Ramadan calls for more festivities, which last for three or four days and this is appropriately called *Eid al Futr* – the Feast of the Break of Fast – and it contains, as one can imagine, all the riches of the earth as far as the table is concerned.

The list of festivities, like the Mediterranean spirit, is joyous and inexhaustible.

Recipes Of The Mediterranean

Gazpacho (Spain)

Gazpacho is a kind of soup which is used as a refreshing drink during the hot months in Spain. Apart from the familiar sharp, earthy *gazpacho* which is made with tomatoes and other summer vegetables, there is also a *Gazpacho Blanco* in Andalusia, with a bridal white appearance which is made mainly with blanched almonds, garlic and morsels of fruit floating on its surface. Either way it makes an exquisite summer lunch.

1 thick, stale slice of bread, crustless
Water
1 lb (450 g) ripe tomatoes, peeled, de-seeded and
 chopped
3 in (7½ cm) piece cucumber, peeled
1 medium onion, peeled and chopped
1 green or red pepper, de-seeded and chopped
2 cloves garlic, peeled and chopped
3 tablespoons olive oil
1 tablespoon wine vinegar
Salt and black pepper
4–5 fresh leaves of mint, finely chopped or a large pinch
 dried mint
1 pt (600 ml) cold water

Soak bread in some water for 10 minutes, squeeze it and place it in a liquidiser with the rest of the ingredients apart from the water and mint. Blend until smooth. Empty into a decorative bowl, dilute with 1 pt (600 ml) water, add mint, mix and chill. Just before serving, float in some ice cubes. With it, offer small bowls of finely chopped onion, pepper and cucumber if you wish.

Serves 4–6

HUMMUS BI TAHINA (MIDDLE EAST)

Hummus is the Middle East's appetiser *par excellence*. Hummus can be served as a dip with fresh bread or *pitta*, or as a sauce with grilled chicken or kebabs. It can be stored in the refrigerator for 3–4 days. Do not use tinned chickpeas, as the result is very poor compared to the authentic dish.

8 oz (225 g) chickpeas, picked clean and soaked
    overnight
2 cloves garlic, peeled and chopped
3 tablespoons tahina paste
1½ lemons
1½ teaspoons ground cummin
4 tablespoons vegetable oil
½ pt (300 ml) chickpea cooking liquid (2 teacups)
Salt and black pepper

Garnish:
1–2 tablespoons olive or vegetable oil
A little cayenne pepper or paprika

Wash the chickpeas and strain. Bring to the boil with plenty of water and skim, then cover and cook until soft. (In a pressure cooker this will take 20 minutes, one and a half hours otherwise). Strain, reserving the cooking liquid.

Add the remaining ingredients to the chickpeas and blend in a liquidiser in two batches. The result should be grainy, and of a runny consistency. Adjust seasoning and blend again briefly.

Pour onto a flat platter. Sprinkle on the oil and the cayenne decoratively in zig-zag patterns before serving.

Serves 6–8

CAPONATA

AUBERGINE IN SWEET AND SOUR SAUCE (SICILY/MALTA)

A dish full of summer memories, that can be served as a first course or as part of an *hors d'oeuvres*. Like all aubergine-olive oil dishes its flavours should be allowed to amalgamate and it is best when served at room temperature.

1½ lbs (675 g) aubergines, trimmed and sliced in thick
  rounds
¼ pt (150 ml) vegetable oil
1 medium onion, finely sliced
5 tablespoons olive oil
3 sticks celery, trimmed, washed and finely chopped
8 oz (225 g) tomatoes, peeled and chopped
3 tablespoons wine vinegar
½ teaspoon origano
1 teaspoon sugar
4 oz (110 g) green olives
1 tablespoon capers, strained
Salt and black pepper

Immerse the aubergines in lightly salted water for 30
minutes. Rinse, squeezing them to extract their bit-
ter juices, and dry. Cut into cubes and deep fry in
the hot vegetable oil until light golden. Drain on
absorbent paper.

Brown the onion in hot olive oil, add the celery
and tomatoes and fry together for 2 minutes. Add
the rest of the ingredients (except the aubergines)
and cook for 8–10 minutes until the sauce thickens.
Add the aubergines, mix well and cook for 3–4 more
minutes. Allow to cool before serving, but do not
refrigerate.

Serve 6

Horiatiki Salata

A Peasant Salad (Greece)

This salad combines most items we associate with the Mediterranean: large scarlet tomatoes, cucumber, sweet peppers, onions, olives and white sheep's or goat's cheese. Eaten in the blistering heat, under the shade of an olive tree, it can make a wonderful meal by itself.

8 oz (225 g) tomatoes, washed, dried and quartered
2 in (5 cm) piece of peeled cucumber, sliced in discs
1/2 a small onion, sliced finely
1 sweet green pepper, cored, de-seeded and sliced
8 large black olives (preferably the heart-shaped Kalamata variety)
4 oz (110 g) Feta cheese, cubed
Large pinch of origano
5 tablespoons olive oil
Salt

Mix all the ingredients in a large bowl, toss lightly and serve immediately.

Serves 4

COQUILLES SAINT-JACQUES A LA PROVENÇALE

SCALLOPS FRIED WITH GARLIC (FRANCE)

Scallops fried in olive oil with a hint of garlic and with parsley added just before serving make a deliciously appetising dish. As scallops are quite rich I always add either cultivated mushrooms or a few *chanterelles* when I can find them and some sliced sweet pepper, either green or red.

8 scallops, shelled, washed and strained
1 oz (25 g) flour
5 tablespoons olive oil
8–10 oz (225–275 g) firm mushrooms, washed and dried
1 small green or red pepper, de-seeded and sliced
1 clove garlic, crushed
2 tablespoons finely chopped parsley
Salt and black pepper

Remove corals and slice each scallop horizontally in 2 discs. Toss lightly in flour and fry gently in 2 tablespoons of hot oil for 1 minute on either side. Add corals once scallops have been turned over. Remove from the pan. Add 3 more tablespoons olive oil to the frying pan and sauté the mushrooms and pepper for 4 minutes. Put scallops back, add garlic, parsley and seasoning; toss over gentle heat for 2 minutes and serve.

Serves 4

CALAMARES EN SU TINTA

SQUID CASSEROLE WITH THEIR INK
(SPAIN)

If you like squid this is one of the most delicious dishes made with it, with variations all round the Mediterranean.

2 lbs (1 kg) squid (large squid are well suited for the dish)
1 lb (450 g) onions chopped
2 cloves garlic, finely chopped
4–5 tablespoons olive oil or vegetable oil
¼ pt (150 ml) dry white wine
5 tablespoons water
Salt and black pepper
2 tablespoons finely chopped parsley

Pull the heads of the squid away from their bodies; cut horizontally under the eyes and reserve the tentacles only; empty the body, extract the silver thread-like bag of ink attached to the innards and reserve; skin body, particularly if the squids are large; slice bodies in 1 in/2½ cm rings. Wash squid meticulously to remove grit and strain. Fry the onions and garlic in the hot oil until glistening, then add squid and fry together for 3–4 minutes. Pour in the wine and then the water; add seasoning, and the reserved ink bags, cover and cook gently for 30–40 minutes, according to size, stirring occasionally. Add the parsley towards the end.

Serves 4–6

DOLMATHAKIA AVGOLEMONO

STUFFED VINE LEAVES (GREECE)

There cannot be a family celebration in Greece without the green presence of stuffed vine leaves on the table. This version with egg and lemon sauce is the most celebratory and should aways be served hot.

*8 oz (225 g) fresh vine leaves (about 48) or 1 packet of
    preserved ones*
1 oz (25 g) butter
1 pt (600 ml) hot water

Stuffing:
*4 oz (110 g) long-grain rice, soaked for 10 minutes,
    washed and strained*
2 large onions, thickly grated
1 lb (450 g) minced beef or lamb
2 oz (50 g) pine kernels
3 tablespoons fresh herbs, such as parsley or dill
Salt and black pepper

Avgolemono Egg and Lemon Sauce:
3 eggs
Juice of 2 lemons
1 teaspoon cornflour
5 tablespoons cooking liquid

Blanch the vine leaves in lightly salted boiling water for 1 minute and strain. If using preserved ones, rinse them to get rid of excess salt and plunge them in a bowl of hot water for 5 minutes; rinse again and strain.

Mix the stuffing ingredients in a bowl. Line the base of a wide saucepan with 3–4 vine leaves to prevent the *dolmathes* from sticking. Trim each leaf of its stalk and place a teaspoonful of stuffing near its serrated base, uneven side upwards. Fold stem ends over it, then both edges inwards and roll into a sausage-like shape. Place in the saucepan, in layered, tight circles, loose end underneath. Add seasoning and butter. Place an inverted small plate on top in order to keep them in place. Pour the hot water in, cover and cook gently for 50 minutes. Let it stand away from heat for 5 minutes before adding the sauce.

Beat the eggs and lemon juice, add cornflour and beat together. Add slowly a few tablespoons of the hot (but not boiling) liquid, beating continuously. Pour the egg and lemon mixture slowly over the *dolmathes* and rotate the saucepan to amalgamate it. Return to a very gentle heat for 3–4 minutes in order to cook the cornflour a little, but on no account should you allow it to boil. Allow 8–10 *dolmathes* per person for a main course or 2–3 for an appetiser.

Osso Buco Alla Romana

Roman Casserole Of Shin Of Veal
(Italy)

Osso buco are 1 in (2½ cm) thick slices, cut horizontally from veal shin with the marrow nestling in the central bone. Special tiny spoons are sometimes offered in Italy for eating the marrow, which is a real delicacy. It is important for the flavour of the dish that a good stock is made beforehand, using pieces of marrow bone which any butcher will provide.

This Roman version is served with spinach and sautéed potatoes.

4 pieces of shin of veal, about 2½ lb (1125 g)
4 tablespoons olive oil
½ oz (15 g) butter
¼ pt (150 ml) dry white wine
1 pt (600 ml) stock
3 sprigs fresh basil or *a piece of orange peel*
Salt and black pepper

Wash and dry meat. Heat the oil and butter in a saucepan that will accommodate the *osso buco* pieces in one layer, and fry on both sides until light golden. Pour the wine all over and then the stock and add the basil and seasoning. Cover and cook very gently for 1½ hours or more until the meat is very tender. Turn the meat over 2–3 times, being careful not to spill or lose the marrow.

Serves 4

DATE TAGINE

MEAT CASSEROLE WITH FRUIT
(MOROCCO)

In Morocco a *tagine* is a casserole of meat or poultry with fruit, but in Tunisia it is a baked dish of vegetables, meat, or fish with eggs added on top, either whole or lightly beaten.

2 lb (1 kg) boneless leg of lamb, cubed
2 tablespoons olive oil
1 large onion, chopped
1/4 teaspoon ground ginger
1/2 teaspoon turmeric
1 teaspoon coriander powder
1/2 teaspoon black pepper or 1/4 teaspoon cayenne pepper
1 pt (600 ml) hot water
Salt
8 oz (225 g) dates, stoned
2 tablespoons fresh chopped coriander

Wash and dry the meat. Brown it in the hot oil, then add onion and a few minutes later the spices. Lower the heat and sauté together for 2–3 minutes. Add the hot water and a little salt, then cover and cook for 45 minutes until the meat is tender, stirring occasionally to prevent sticking. Add the dates and the fresh coriander, mix, cover and cook for 10 more minutes. Serve with rice or *couscous*.

Serves 6

ARNAKI FRICASSEE

LAMB WITH COS LETTUCE CASSEROLE
(GREECE)

With the first whiff of spring and the arrival of
Easter (and of the new baby lambs), this is the
Sunday lunch in most Greek homes.

1 medium-sized, boned shoulder of lamb, trimmed of fat
2 bunches of spring onions, trimmed and chopped
3 tablespoons vegetable oil
1½ pt (900 ml) hot water
Salt
3 tablespoons chopped fresh dill
3 large cos lettuces, washed and shredded
3 eggs
Juice of 2 large lemons

Cube, wash and strain meat. Sauté the onions in the
oil, add the meat and sauté together for 3–4 minutes.
Add water and salt, cover and cook for 40 minutes
until the meat is tender but not falling apart. Add
the dill and lettuces and mix, then cover and cook
gently for 10 minutes. Let the dish stand for 5
minutes before adding the sauce.

Lightly beat the eggs with the lemon juice and add
3–4 tablespoons of the hot (but not boiling) cooking
liquid from the lamb gradually while beating all the
time. Pour the sauce over the contents of the casserole and stir until well amalgamated. Return to a very
gentle heat for 1–2 minutes, just to warm through.

Serves 6

POULET AUX OLIVES

CHICKEN CASSEROLE WITH OLIVES
(FRANCE)

Olives are used with poultry, meat and fish casseroles all round the Mediterranean. This chicken dish from the South of France can also be found in Greece, Italy and Morocco, with minor variations.

1 chicken, jointed, about 3 lb (1.5 kg)
5 tablespoons vegetable oil
1 medium onion, chopped
2 cloves garlic, peeled and crushed
1 glass white wine
3–4 medium tomatoes, peeled and chopped
½ pt (300 ml) hot water
Salt and black pepper
12 black olives, rinsed
2 tablespoons chopped parsley

Wash and dry chicken pieces. Brown in the hot oil on both sides and reserve. Fry the onion in the same saucepan and when it glistens add the garlic and sauté together for 2 minutes. Return the chicken pieces, pour the wine on top, add the tomatoes, water and seasoning, then cover and cook for 45 minutes. Add the olives and parsley and cook for 10 more minutes. Serve with rice or boiled new potatoes.

Serves 4–6

Ryzogalo

RICE PUDDING (GREECE/TURKEY)

A creamy delicate contrast to a robust and spicy main course.

2 oz (50 g) pudding rice, washed and strained
¼ pt (150 ml) hot water
½ pt (300 ml) milk
1½ oz (40 g) sugar
1 teaspoon cornflour diluted in a ½ cup of milk
3–4 drops pure vanilla essence or rosewater
1 egg yolk, lightly beaten
½ teaspoon cinnamon for sprinkling on top

Cook the rice in the water until most of it has been absorbed. Add the milk, mix and cook gently, half-covered, for 25 minutes. Then add the sugar, corn-flour, vanilla or rosewater and cook for 5 more minutes. Remove from the heat and let it cool slightly. Add the egg yolk slowly, stirring until well amalgamated, then return to a very gentle heat for just a few seconds. Pour into small bowls immediately and sprinkle cinnamon on top. It can be eaten hot or cold.

Serves 4

GRANITA DI COCOMERO

WATER-MELON ICE (ITALY)

If Italy is the queen of ices, Sicily is indisputably the queen of water ices. The flavours of *Granite* are inexhaustible, from coffee to all kinds of fruit – lemons, strawberries, peaches and many more. Ices have had a long history in Italy, and are as popular today as with the early Romans, who would dispatch their low-ranking soldiers to fetch ice from the Apennines.

Water ices are extremely easy to make and one can improvise with whatever fruit is in season. They need no beating while freezing, but bring them out of the freezer 10–15 minutes before they are to be served as they become quite solid.

12 oz (350 g) water-melon flesh, seeds removed
7 oz (200 g) sugar
½ pt (300 ml) water

Garnish:
Mint leaves

Liquidise the water-melon or press through a coarse sieve. Dissolve the sugar in the water and boil for 10 minutes until thickened. When cool mix well with the water-melon and freeze for 2–3 hours. Serve in tall glasses with 1–2 fresh mint leaves on top.

Serves 6

ACKNOWLEDGEMENTS

The Mediterraneanness of this little book has been enriched by the enthusiasm and knowledge of a number of good friends, and although the limited space would not allow me to bring them all in I must mention and thank my friends Vera Kyriakou, Alicia Rios Ivars, Ange de Vena, Lala Isla and Sami Zubaida. The execution of the book owes a great deal to Graeme Salaman who inspires and nags (gently, I hasten to add) at home.

I am also grateful to the valuable sources from which I took the liberty of quoting.